Contents

Words that appear in **bold** in the text are explained in the glossary on page 46.

1 Introducing China

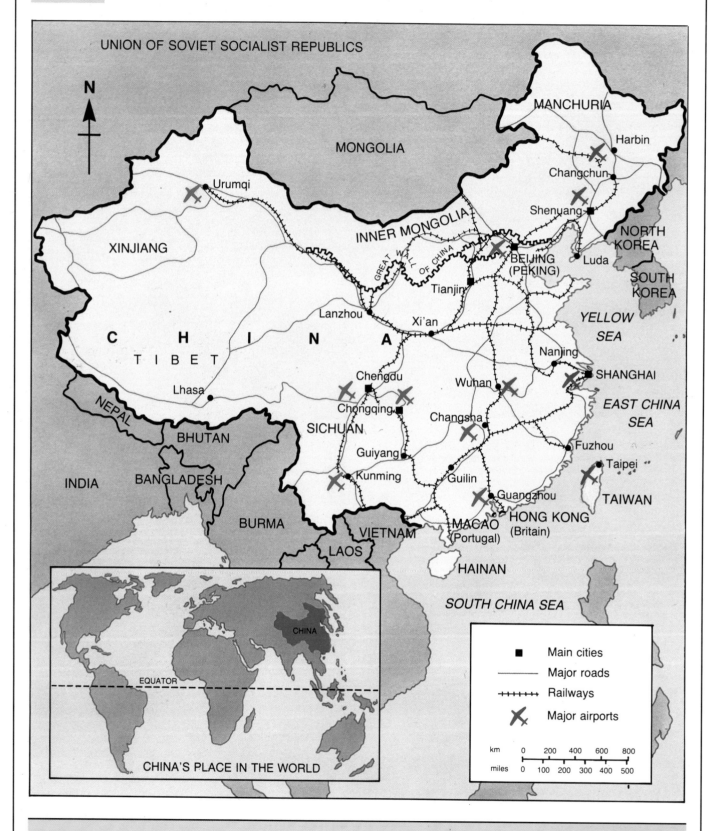

UNION OF SOVIET SOCIALIST REPUBLICS

N

MANCHURIA

MONGOLIA

Harbin

Changchun

Urumqi

INNER MONGOLIA

Shenyang

NORTH KOREA

XINJIANG

GREAT WALL OF CHINA

BEIJING (PEKING)

Luda

SOUTH KOREA

Tianjin

C H I N A

Lanzhou

Xi'an

YELLOW SEA

T I B E T

Nanjing

SHANGHAI

Chengdu

Wuhan

EAST CHINA SEA

Lhasa

Chongqing

Changsha

NEPAL

SICHUAN

Fuzhou

BHUTAN

Guiyang

Taipei

INDIA

BANGLADESH

Kunming

Guilin

TAIWAN

Guangzhou

BURMA

VIETNAM

MACAO (Portugal)

HONG KONG (Britain)

LAOS

HAINAN

SOUTH CHINA SEA

CHINA

EQUATOR

CHINA'S PLACE IN THE WORLD

	Main cities
	Major roads
	Railways
	Major airports

km 0   200   400   600   800

miles 0 100 200 300 400 500

COUNTRIES OF THE WORLD

CHINA

Julia Waterlow

with photographs by Richard Sharpley

Illustrated by Peter Bull

Wayland

Titles in this series

Australia	Italy
Canada	Japan
The Caribbean	The Netherlands
China	New Zealand
France	Pakistan
Great Britain	Spain
Greece	The U.S.A.
India	West Germany

Cover *Wheat straw being collected from the road where it has been drying.*

Opposite *A peasant woman in southern China on her way to market.*

First published in 1989 by
Wayland (Publishers) Ltd
61 Western Road, Hove
East Sussex BN3 1JD, England

© Copyright 1989 Wayland (Publishers) Ltd

Editor: Philippa Smith
Series design: Malcolm Smythe
Book design: David Armitage

British Library Cataloguing in Publication Data
Waterlow, Julia
    China. – (Countries of the World).
    1. China – For Schools
    I. Title II. Sharpley, Richard III. Series
    951.05'8

ISBN 1–85210–043–5

Typeset by Lizzie George, Wayland
Printed in Italy by G. Canale and C.S.p.A., Turin
Bound in Belgium by Casterman S.A.

China

Land area: 9,560,000 sq km
Population: 1,080,000,000
(1987)
Capital city: Beijing

Crowds in the evening rush hour in Beijing.

The Chinese call China the 'Middle Kingdom'. For hundreds of years they believed that their country was the middle, or centre, of the civilized world and they took little interest in what lay beyond their borders. Its geography, too, has kept China **isolated** from its neighbours. To the north are great deserts, to the west high mountains and to the east is the South China Sea. More than 2,000 years ago the Chinese started building a huge structure to stop invaders: the famous Great Wall, which runs for about 4,000 km across north China.

China is one of the oldest civilizations in the world. Until about the seventeenth century, Chinese technology was well in advance of that in the West. For example, 1,500 years ago they had invented and were using paper and gunpowder. However, when the West did start to

develop, China's rulers tried to keep out all new foreign ideas. It was only this century that there was any industrial progress. In order to bring in up-to-date technology, China has now become friendly and created trading links with many foreign countries.

Even though China has some of the biggest cities in the world, the majority of the Chinese are still farmers living in the countryside. Most people now have enough to eat but they are very poor compared with those in more developed countries.

Over the last 40 years or so there has been a big improvement in health care and in food production. This has nearly doubled **life expectancy** but has led to a massive population explosion. Much of the huge land area is uninhabitable, so it is very crowded in the parts of China where people are able to live.

2 CHINA

Land and climate

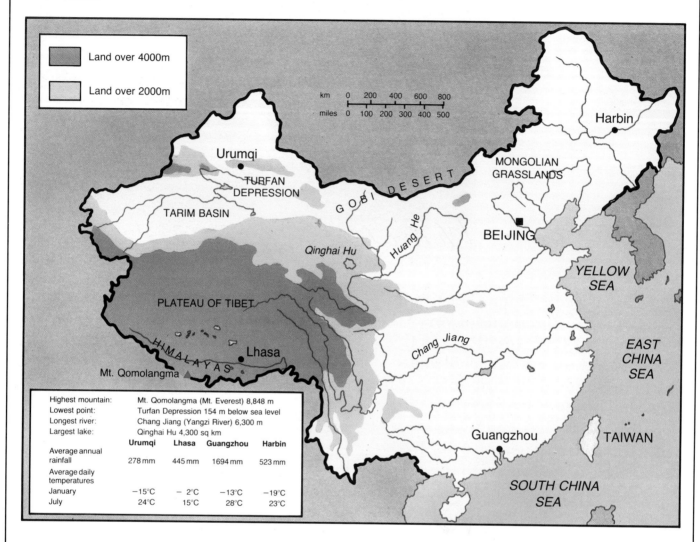

Land over 4000m

Land over 2000m

| km | 0 | 200 | 400 | 600 | 800 |
| miles | 0 | 100 200 | 300 | 400 | 500 |

Harbin

MONGOLIAN GRASSLANDS

GOBI DESERT

Urumqi

TURFAN DEPRESSION

TARIM BASIN

Huang He

BEIJING

Qinghai Hu

YELLOW SEA

PLATEAU OF TIBET

HIMALAYAS

Lhasa

Mt. Qomolangma

Chang Jiang

EAST CHINA SEA

Guangzhou

TAIWAN

SOUTH CHINA SEA

Highest mountain:	Mt. Qomolangma (Mt. Everest) 8,848 m			
Lowest point:	Turfan Depression 154 m below sea level			
Longest river:	Chang Jiang (Yangzi River) 6,300 m			
Largest lake:	Qinghai Hu 4,300 sq km			
	Urumqi	**Lhasa**	**Guangzhou**	**Harbin**
Average annual rainfall	278 mm	445 mm	1694 mm	523 mm
Average daily temperatures				
January	−15°C	− 2°C	−13°C	−19°C
July	24°C	15°C	28°C	23°C

In terms of land area, China is the third largest country in the world. Even though it is such a vast country, about two-thirds of the land is mountains and desert and unsuitable for farming or settlement.

Geographically, China is rather like a staircase. It starts with the high Himalayas, where Mount Qomolangma (Everest) lies, and then steps down to the plateau of Tibet and Qinghai which averages 4,000 m in height. This area is often called 'The Roof of the World' and is very wild, **barren** and cold. To the north of the plateau the land drops steeply to the Tarim Basin. Much of this area is desert, scattered with **oases**. To the east the mountains step down gradually to the hills and plains of eastern China where the two great rivers, the Huang He (Yellow River) and the Chang Jiang (Yangzi River), flow across **fertile** flat land.

The climate in the north and west of China can be quite extreme. Temperatures sometimes fall to - 40 °C in winter and rise to 40 °C in summer. The rainfall is irregular and **droughts** are common. In the far south of China it is warm all the year round. The countryside here is lush and green. **Monsoon** winds bring plenty of rain to the area south of the Chang Jiang.

Above The huge Huang He (Yellow River) passes through the industrial city of Lanzhou.

Right The unusual limestone scenery near Guilin is one of China's most famous tourist attractions.

Below This high plateau is in the far west of China. A few sheep and goats graze on the thin grass.

In the north, icy winds from Siberia blow across the Gobi Desert, bringing loess soil (which is very fine and dusty) and dropping it in the area around the Huang He. This is very fertile soil but easily washed away. The yellow colour of the soil gives the Huang He its name. The Chinese also call this river 'China's Sorrow' because it often floods, washing away crops and villages.

3 Wildlife

The number of wild animals in China has been drastically reduced as more and more land has been cultivated to feed the population. In addition, the Chinese have hunted animals of all kinds for food and medicines. The Government is now making efforts to save the animals and birds by creating wildlife reserves.

The most famous animal in China is the giant panda. This is the symbol for the World Wide Fund for Nature. Pandas are found in the wild areas of Sichuan. Bamboo is their only food and they eat about 20 kg a day. They are finding it difficult to survive because they only eat one special variety of bamboo which is becoming scarce. Pandas are now an **endangered species**.

Above The Siberian tiger lives in the far north of China. There are few left because of hunters.

Left A panda in the protection of Beijing Zoo.

Other wild animals found in China include two types of tiger, the golden monkey, wild deer, the giant **salamander** and the Chinese alligator. The 1,200 species of birds in China include cranes, colourful pheasants and peacocks. The pretty Mandarin duck is native to China. It has the same mate for the whole of its life and so is considered a symbol of love.

The male Mandarin duck is very colourful. Originally from China, these ducks can now be found on lakes in parks around the world.

Many common plants grown in gardens around the world come from China, for example, the rose, the chrysanthemum and the peony.

Some wild animals have been **domesticated** for daily use. In Tibet the tough **yak** is used as a pack animal. Wild horses still exist in some parts of Mongolia but most are now either ridden or pull carts. Camels are also tamed and are used to carry loads across the deserts of the north-west. In tropical south-west China, elephants do the heavy work in the forests.

4 History

Chinese civilization has the longest continuous history of any in the world. For more than 3,000 years China was ruled by a series of **dynasties**, or families headed by emperors. It was first united into one country in 221 BC by a cruel but strong emperor call Qin (pronounced 'chin'), giving China the name we use today. He ordered the building of the Great Wall and a spectacular **tomb** with a clay army of more than 7,000 lifesize men and horses.

Above This 2,000-year-old lifesize warrior and horse are part of the enormous Terracotta (clay) Army, discovered in 1974.

The famous Great Wall of China stretches from the coast for thousands of miles to the west. Much is now in ruins but parts, like this section near Beijing, have been rebuilt.

During the Han dynasty which followed, paper, the **seismograph** and the compass were invented. It was also the time when the ideas of the **philosopher** Confucius became very important and these have affected the Chinese way of life all through history. Over the next few hundred years art, culture, education, technology and philosophy all blossomed. China was one of the most advanced civilizations in the world at that time.

In the thirteenth century the Mongol armies of **Genghis Khan** swept over the Great Wall from the north and took control of China. During the Mongol rule a few Europeans, such as **Marco Polo**, managed to make the long trip overland to China, following the old

Right This illustration shows Genghis Khan and his army capturing a Chinese town. It is taken from a Persian history of Gengis Khan, completed in 1596.

silk trading routes. Their stories of the splendour that they found amazed people in Europe.

From the seventeenth century onwards many Europeans came to buy silk, tea, jade and **porcelain**. The British brought the drug opium into China from India and traded it for Chinese goods. The Chinese emperors tried to stop trade with foreigners, especially the import of opium. This led to the first of the 'Opium Wars' between the British and the Chinese. The Chinese lost and Europeans established settlements on the coast.

The Boxer Uprising of 1900 was a fierce but unsuccessful protest against the presence of foreign powers in China. This picture shows European troops fighting the Boxer rebels in Beijing.

Throughout Chinese history wealth and power belonged to a small number of people who ruthlessly **exploited** the ordinary **peasants**. In 1911, the peasants revolted, finally ending the rule of the great Chinese dynasties.

Sun Yat Sen, who was the leader of the Nationalist Party at this time, declared China a **republic** in 1912. Unfortunately he was unable to unite China and powerful **warlords** with their own armies took control in many areas. Fighting between these warlords continued for several years and the people continued to suffer.

New **revolutionary** ideas were catching on and in 1921 the Chinese Communist Party was formed. The new leader of the Nationalist Party, called Chiang Kai Shek, did not want to share power with the Communists. When Japan invaded China in 1931, instead of fighting the Japanese, Chiang Kai Shek turned his armies on the peasants and workers who formed the Communist Party's 'Red Army'. The Red Army was driven out of its base in the south and began the 'Long March' across China to the north. It was led by Mao Zedong. The Red Army took over a year to cover 12,000 km to its new base. Many men and women died on the way but the Communists gained the support of millions of peasants as they passed through the countryside.

After the Second World War (1939-45) the Communists began to overcome Chiang Kai Shek's forces.

On 1 October 1949, Mao Zedong proclaimed the new People's Republic of China. Property was taken from rich landlords and managed by the ordinary people for the benefit of everyone.

In 1966 Mao Zedong launched the Cultural Revolution, hoping to change every aspect of Chinese life. The next ten years were full of chaos and confusion – many people were killed or sent to work as labourers in the countryside if they criticized the Communist Party. Schools were closed and books and art treasures destroyed.

After Mao Zedong's death in 1976, the Chinese leaders took a fairer and more reasonable outlook and concentrated on improving the country's economy.

Above A statue of peasants and soldiers marching during the Communist Revolution.

Important dates

BC

2000-1000	Ancient Xia and Shang dynasties.
551	The Birth of Confucius.
221-207	The emperor Qin Shi Huang Di unites the Chinese Empire.
206 BC-AD 220	Han dynasty expands boundaries and centralizes government.

AD

618-907	The Tang dynasty brings artistic and cultural development. Buddhism flourishes.
960-1279	The Song dynasty introduces political and economic reforms.
1279-1368	The Mongols invade and set up a foreign dynasty.
1368-1644	The Ming dynasty.
1644	The beginning of the Qing dynasty, invaders from Manchuria.
1839-1842	The Opium Wars.
1911	Corrupt Qing dynasty overthrown by the followers of Sun Yat Sen.
1912	The Chinese Republic is declared.
1921	Chinese Communist Party formed.
1931	The Japanese invade Manchuria.
1934-35	The Long March.
1945-49	Civil War.
1949	Mao Zedong declares the People's Republic of China.
1966	The Cultural Revolution begins.
1976	Mao Zedong dies.
1977	Deng Xiaoping becomes Senior Vice-Premier and effectively the ruler of China. Economic but not political reforms follow.
1989	Students protest for more democratic government. Many are shot and imprisoned.

5 The people today

Over one billion (1,000,000,000) people live in China, about a quarter of the world's population. In every 100 people 93 are Han Chinese, the original Chinese, and the remainder are made up of a great variety of different peoples from 55 **minority** races and groups.

There are the Zhuang, the largest minority who live in the south; the Hui who are **Muslims**; the Uygurs living on the western border with the USSR; the **Buddhist** Tibetans who live on the high plateau; the Dai who live on the sub-tropical borders near Laos. Many more smaller minority groups live in the south-west. Several have kept their own language, colourful dress, traditional customs and religion. These minority peoples inhabit about half China's land area, but tend to live in remote or border regions.

Most of China's Han population live in the fertile hills and plains in the east of the country, although several million have been sent to work in far distant towns and cities such as Lhasa in Tibet. About 8 out of 10 Chinese still live and work in the countryside.

Above This farmer lives in Guizhon province in southern China.

Right A crowd of Han Chinese. Most Chinese people belong to the Han group.

Above These children belong to the Tajik minority from the far west of China.

Below A one-child family in Beijing.

The population is increasing rapidly: about twenty-five babies are born every minute. The Government is trying hard to slow the population growth. Parents are encouraged to have only one child, although people from the minority groups do not have to follow this rule. Families receive bonus payments, higher pensions, and better housing and schooling if they have only one child.

It is difficult for the Government to enforce birth control because traditionally the Chinese have always had large families. In the towns birth control has been successful, but in the country there are still families with many children because they need them to help work on the land.

6 Cities

Modern buildings rise up behind the roofs of the Forbidden City in Beijing.

In China there are thirteen cities with a population of more than 2 million people. Cities are usually very crowded and **polluted**, bustling with people and bicycles. Old buildings have been demolished to be replaced by wide streets, big concrete blocks of flats and industrial buildings.

Beijing (Peking), with a population of about 9 million, first became the capital of China under the Mongols.

About 500 years ago a magnificent palace was built, known as the 'Forbidden City' because only the emperor and his staff and family were allowed in. This huge complex is in the centre of Beijing and the area around still has the old layout of small single-storey houses in narrow lanes called *hutongs*. In front of the Forbidden City the Government has built the biggest public square in the world – Tiananmen Square.

Beijing is a criss-cross of streets running north to south and east to west. If the Chinese are giving directions, they say 'turn north' or 'turn south' not 'turn left' or 'turn right'!

Shanghai is one of the biggest cities in the world with a population of 12 million. Being near the sea and the Chang Jiang, which reaches far inland, it is an important port. Industry and business thrive and it is the most fashionable city in China. It has a long history of contact with Europeans, who once controlled trade here.

Above New apartment blocks are springing up everywhere to house the huge population of the cities.

Left Crowds of people on Nanjing Lu, the main shopping street in Shanghai.

In the south of China is Guangzhou (Canton), another city with historical European ties. There has been a lot of foreign investment here recently and twice-yearly trade fairs are held. Many of the Chinese who live in nearby **Hong Kong** originally came from Guangzhou. They regularly make trips back to mainland China to visit their relatives and bring with them the latest Western goods.

7 Home life

Above A family working in rice fields outside their house.

Whether they live in the town or the country, each family's home usually has only one or two rooms. Often one room doubles as their sitting room and bedroom; some facilities, like the kitchen, are shared with other families. Only new flats in the cities have bathrooms and toilets, so most people use a communal toilet and bath house. Central heating is rare, but in the north some houses have brick beds called *kangs*, heated by stoves so that they stay warm day and night.

In the countryside most houses still have no running water and it has to be fetched every day from a well or a river. Houses are quite different in some of the minority areas. In Mongolia the **nomadic** families live in yurts. These are round tents which can be moved in the summer when the animals are taken to new pastures.

Families do not have many possessions. Inside the house or flat the furniture is very simple and the floors are stone, earth or concrete.

Often posters and family photographs are hung on the wall and some people have a radio or a television. Many houses face on to a communal courtyard where washing is hung and pot plants are grown.

The lack of space in which to live means that people like to go outside as much as possible. When the weather is warm enough they sit out on the street on small bamboo stools doing their washing, chatting or watching the world go by.

Every day the Chinese get up early, between 5.30 and 6.30 am. Many take regular exercise before they go to school or work. They all have an early lunch, perhaps at 11.00 or 12.00, and come home for supper around 5.30 pm. Most people are in bed by about 9.00 pm.

Above *Some nomadic people in north-west China live in tents called yurts.*

Above *Few people have running water in their homes: this man is washing his clothes with water from a well in the street.*

Right *The courtyard of an old house in the city.*

8 Growing up in China

Both parents usually work and so small children go to day centres or are looked after by grandparents who live in the same house. All three generations often live together and there are strong family ties. Parents do not have much spare money to spend so, although children are given a lot of attention, they do not have as many toys as those in the West. Nor do they have much free time because they have to study hard for school or help their parents in the house or in the fields. When they do go out to play it is usually in the communal courtyard, in the street or in a nearby park.

Above Basketball is often played at school.

Below Chinese children are expected to help their parents. This boy is mending fishing nets.

A mother feeding her child at the side of the street. Chinese people spend much of their time outdoors because their houses are quite small.

Below A girl does her homework in a courtyard shared by several families.

Most children and adults go to school or work six days a week and there are few holidays. Holidays are spent at home, visiting relations or occasionally going on trips arranged by schools or places of work.

Everyone in China belongs to a 'work unit' which organizes and provides all the things they and their children need as they grow up. A work unit could include, for example, everyone who works at a particular factory, bus company or a village in the countryside. In addition to their pay, the workers are provided with cheap or free housing, schools and medical care. There may also be recreation facilities such as a basketball court or a cinema.

When children leave school, they do not apply for jobs but are told what their work will be and where it will be. Sometimes their job will be in a different province and then they do not often see their family. Due to the shortage of housing, single people living away from their families have to live in big dormitories.

9 Education

Chinese children start school when they are 6 or 7 years old and must go to school for nine years. After primary school, when they are about 11 or 12, they go to secondary school. If they are clever enough, they can stay on after the nine compulsory years to study further.

Children at a secondary school in Lanzhou. The children pay close attention to their teacher.

In the classroom children learn eight basic subjects including Chinese, mathematics and politics. Physical exercise is considered very important and at the beginning of the day at school there is usually some group exercise. They are expected to work hard and they have to learn communal responsibility, obedience, politeness and to be loyal to their country. Children in a Chinese classroom are very well behaved!

Exercise-time for students of a Uygur primary school in western China.

More children are now learning technical skills, such as engineering, building and metalworking, which will be useful immediately they leave school. English is taught in many schools as a second language. In the minority areas the students have classes in their own languages as well as in Chinese.

School starts at about 7.45 am and finishes at about 4.00 pm, with a two-hour break in the day when children go home for lunch. After school there is always homework to do. They go to school six days a week with Sundays as their day off.

During the year, children have two five-week holidays. In the rural areas there are fewer schools, they are less well equipped and pupils do not attend school regularly. The parents think it is more useful for the children to help work in the fields than to attend school every day.

Only about 1 in 20 secondary school students can hope to get to university or college owing to the limited number of places available. Competition is strong and students have to work extremely hard. Success in exams before leaving school is all important.

10 Shops and shopping

Shops come in all shapes and sizes, but big department stores and street markets are found in every Chinese town. The department stores sell a wide range of general household items – clothes, shoes and even musical instruments – all at prices controlled by the Government. Here the Chinese can get bicycles, radios, watches and televisions, which are the main luxuries they save money to buy. Most of the products are made in China because imported foreign goods are very expensive.

Below A woman uses an abacus (a frame with beads on rods or wires) to add a bill in a restaurant. The Chinese have used abacuses for counting for over a thousand years.

Above People buy fresh vegetables every day in markets.

The market and open street stalls are where people usually buy their food. There is always a big display of vegetables. Sometimes there are heaps of cabbages on the pavement in the winter or water-melons in the summer. Some markets sell more unusual items such as snakes, frogs, tortoises, and dogs, all of which are eaten.

Rather than buying ready-made clothes, many people buy cloth and make their own clothes because it is cheaper. Older men and women generally wear blue or green jackets and trousers, but younger people are beginning to wear more colourful and Western-style clothes. Parents like to dress their small children in bright, cheerful outfits.

There is always a shop or a stall selling medicines. It is possible to buy modern drugs but many Chinese believe in traditional medicines which have been used for thousands of years. Herbs, plant roots, powdered deer antlers and dried snake are among some of the items sold as cures for illnesses.

Streets and pavements are full of traders: it is not unusual to see a barber set up a chair in the open, a watch repairer at work, and even a dentist attending to patients at a table or chair on the pavement.

Left This Tibetan man sells traditional medicines.

Below Modern department stores are found in every town and city.

11 Food

Above Making noodles by twisting and spinning the dough is an art.

Left Strings of noodles hanging out to dry in the sun.

The Chinese food usually served in the West is Cantonese, but each region of China has its own specialities. Beijing is famous for its tasty roast duck and in Sichuan the people eat hot spicy dishes. Food is considered one of the main pleasures of life in China.

In the north of China the people tend to eat **noodles** with their meals and in the south, rice. Meat is still a luxury in some poorer parts of China and they may just have vegetables with their noodles or rice. There are many types of vegetables including bamboo shoots, beansprouts and protein-rich soya beans which are made into *doufu* (beancurd). Most Chinese do not like eating dairy products such as cheese or milk.

Because in the past there have been widespread **famines**, the Chinese have learnt to eat every kind of animal and every part of the animal. Some of these have become delicacies; for example camel's paw, ducks' feet and fish lips. Although the Chinese will eat just about anything that moves, the most common meat is pork.

Normally the Chinese steam or fry their food as these methods of cooking do not require much fuel. The food is steamed in baskets or fried in big curved pans called woks. It is always eaten with chopsticks and the rice is served in small bowls. They have also developed many methods of preserving food – this is very useful because there are few fridges.

At breakfast rice porridge is often eaten. At other meals there are usually several different dishes served at once from which each person takes a little. Soup is served at the end of a meal. Tea, without milk or sugar, is the most common drink but the Chinese also like beer and wine. On special occasions they have banquets with as many as twenty different dishes.

Right Chinese food is usually cooked in large, curved metal pans called woks.

Below Families eating at an outdoor food stall.

12 Sport and leisure

Above Chinese chess is very popular and often played outdoors.

Below People practising taiji in their local park.

Although the Chinese have little spare time, they enjoy a wide variety of sports and hobbies. Popular sports are basketball, table-tennis, badminton and football. All these can be played without much equipment. Outside factories, offices, schools and houses, and in parks, there are basketball nets and table-tennis tables ready for games during breaks.

Early in the morning many people go to the parks to practise taiji, or shadow-boxing, a form of gentle exercise with slow movements. The younger people tend to prefer the more active sword-play, or kungfu.

The parks are great meeting and exercise places. They are always crowded with people. Many come to have a game of cards, to play Chinese chess or to listen to singers and storytellers. Groups of old men like to chat to friends, or sit by their caged birds listening to them sing. In the spring children enjoy flying kites.

Indoors, everyone likes listening to the radio or watching television. Often there may be twenty or more people watching the set together in a public place because many families cannot afford their own television. Now that most Chinese children can read and write, street libraries, where people can sit on little stools and read books, are always full.

Young people like to go to the cinema and Western-style dancing is a growing hobby. Acrobatics, juggling, conjurers and puppets are all very popular. If they can afford it, the Chinese love to take photographs. At all tourist spots, squares and parks there are photographers who take pictures for those who do not own a camera.

Above A street library where young people come to read books.

Right An old man sits and listens to his caged birds singing.

13 Religion and traditions

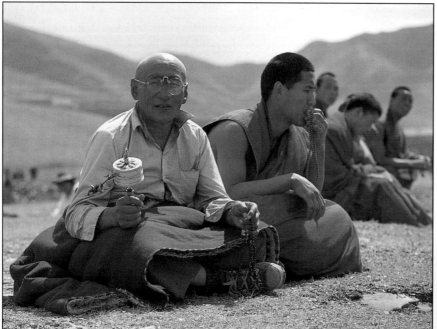

Left A Tibetan Buddhist swings a prayer wheel. He is sitting with a group of monks.

Below A woman kneels in front of an altar in a Chinese Buddhist temple.

Religion does not form an important part of most Chinese people's lives today. They are essentially practical people although some old beliefs do remain. Some of the older Chinese and minority peoples are religious; the Hui minority and the people of the north-west are Muslims, and in parts of China there are Christians. Nowadays the Communist Government is allowing some religious freedom, but it is not encouraged.

The two philosophies of Daoism and Confucianism, together with Buddhism which used to be the main religion in China, have shaped Chinese society and thinking over the centuries. Buddhism is still actively practised in Tibet, where there used to be thousands of monasteries and the people would travel great distances across barren mountains on **pilgrimages**. Some beautiful monasteries and temples remain despite the destruction of many during the Cultural Revolution.

There are many traditions in China. One is to name each year after one of twelve animals. For example, 1988 was the year of the dragon, a symbol of good fortune. Since the traditional Chinese calendar is based upon **lunar months**, the new year is not on a fixed day but varies each year, falling sometime in late January or early February.

The New Year festival, which is the main celebration in China, lasts for several days. Out on the streets everyone lets off fireworks. They dress in their best clothes, visit relations, have open-air shows and enjoy good food. Red paper decorations are made, as red is believed to bring good luck. Chinese communities abroad, such as those in San Francisco, USA and Toronto in Canada, also keep these traditions.

Other traditional Chinese festivals are the Qing Ming festival when **ancestors** are honoured, the Moon festival when paper lanterns are lit, and the Dragon Boat festival. There are also family celebrations such as weddings, and official public holidays when everyone has the day off.

Below A long boat with a dragon's head is being prepared for racing in the Dragon Boat Festival in southern China.

14 Writing and language

Chinese writing is made up of 'characters' – these are groups of brush or pen strokes. Every spoken **syllable** is represented by a character and each character has its own meaning. Although there are more than 50,000 characters, most children will be taught about 3,000 to begin with. There is no alphabet and so no spelling to learn, but instead each individual character has to be learnt by heart. They have to be written very exactly because if one brush stroke is put in a different place, the character takes on a completely new meaning (see diagram 1).

Chinese characters are more than 3,000 years old and come from ancient 'ideograms', a type of picture writing. Some characters still look like the things they represent (see diagram 2), but most are far more complicated. To create new words, two characters are put together: for example, 'telephone' in Chinese is made up of the character for 'electric' and the character for 'talk'. 'Aeroplane' combines the characters for 'flying' and 'machine'.

1 Just changing one brush stroke can alter the meaning of a character.

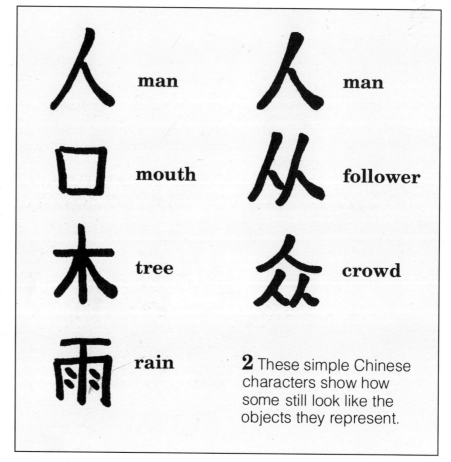

2 These simple Chinese characters show how some still look like the objects they represent.

Traditionally Chinese writing started on the right and ran up the page from bottom to top, but modern books and newspapers are now printed from left to right.

The spoken language varies from region to region so that in the north they pronounce a character in a completely different way from people in the south. However, the written character means the same to all Chinese and therefore they can always communicate by writing.

Left Writing a poem in Chinese, using a brush in the traditional way. The art of writing, or calligraphy, has always been highly respected in China.

Below Posters giving information, advice and news are often pasted up on walls.

15 Culture and the arts

Above A Tang dynasty Buddhist cave painting at Dunhuang in north-west China. The dry climate in this region has preserved this beautiful painting perfectly.

Like the history of China, culture and art go back for hundreds of years. During the Cultural Revolution everything that was not directly concerned with Communism was banned and priceless collections of books and art were destroyed. However, there is now a revival and interest in all forms of art, both traditional and modern. The young Chinese people are also influenced by foreign ideas because there are now opportunities for them to hear music, read books and see films from the West.

Right A classical Ming dynasty garden in Suzhou, near Shanghai.

Two of the best known traditional Chinese arts are painting and calligraphy, both of which use brush and ink. In painting, the quality of the brushwork is the most important feature. The painter is supposed to work from memory so that the picture is not life-like but captures the spirit of the subject. Classical paintings always have characters added to the picture to explain the artist's idea.

Ceramics and pottery have an even older history. The Chinese developed porcelain and china a long time before the Europeans. Gardens too, built by rich officials, were designed with great artistry. They have no flowers or fountains, just rocks, water, a few trees and **pavilions**. Modern parks still use some of these ideas.

Poetry and prose have always been popular. Today over two thousand of the Tang dynasty (618-907) poets are still read. Classical stories written hundreds of years ago are known by many children, a famous one being *The Water Margin* whose hero is a Chinese-style Robin Hood.

The Chinese also enjoy music. There are popular modern songs as well as music played on the traditional Chinese violin. In classical opera the actors wear elaborate masks and costumes and they sing with high-pitched piercing voices.

Above A Uygur girl dances and sings. Behind, a man is playing the traditional Chinese violin.

Left Bamboo is often chosen as the subject for traditional Chinese painting. The artist has added characters to describe his picture.

16 Farming

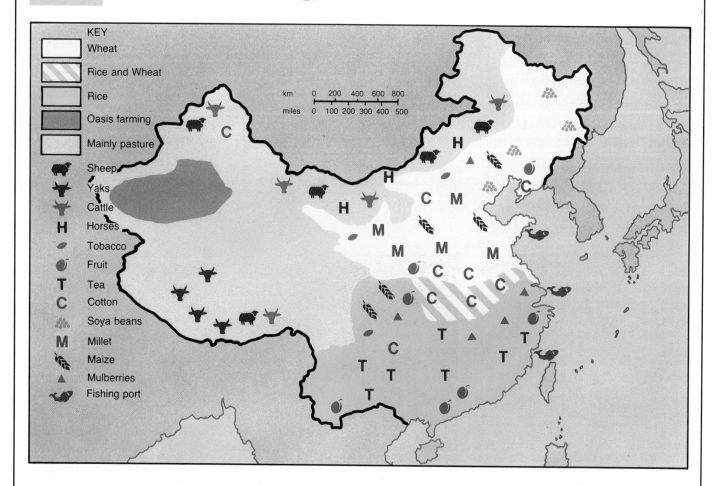

KEY
- Wheat
- Rice and Wheat
- Rice
- Oasis farming
- Mainly pasture
- Sheep
- Yaks
- Cattle
- **H** Horses
- Tobacco
- Fruit
- **T** Tea
- **C** Cotton
- Soya beans
- **M** Millet
- Maize
- ▲ Mulberries
- Fishing port

km 0 200 400 600 800
miles 0 100 200 300 400 500

Despite China's size, it is only possible to use about one-sixth of the land for crops, the rest being grassland, desert or mountains. Every piece of useful land has to be farmed to feed the enormous population.

The most important food crops are wheat, grown in the north, and rice which is grown in the warmer and wetter south. Vegetables are grown all over China and nearly every family in the country has a small vegetable plot. There is little spare land for pasture and so the Chinese raise animals that can **forage** for themselves, such as pigs, chickens and ducks.

There are grazing lands in north and west China. On the Tibetan plateau yak are raised, in Xinjiang sheep are important and in Mongolia herds of horses roam the grasslands.

Most farmwork is done by hand and fields are ploughed with the help of an ox, buffalo or horse. Although tractors are slowly being introduced, they are too expensive for many work units to buy and often unsuitable for working on terraced hillsides.

Most of the fish eaten in China are freshwater fish. Many villages have a fish pond, or the fish are caught daily from rivers or lakes. Many of the forests in China have disappeared over the years, being cleared for crops and used for fuel. The Government is encouraging replanting schemes all over the country.

All land is owned by the Government. Some farmers work on **state farms** and others rent land. In return they have to grow a certain amount for the Government but they can sell any **surplus** in the markets.

Right A man plants rice shoots. Rice needs plenty of water to grow.

Below Buffalo are used for most of the work in the rice fields.

17 Industry

Industrialization in China started much later than in other countries. Although output is increasing, industry faces problems of old-fashioned machinery and overmanning. China has tried to be **self-sufficient** but recently there has been a big growth in imported foreign machinery and **expertise** to help modernize and improve technology. Most industries and businesses are still state owned but the Government is now encouraging **private enterprise**.

The Chinese were the first people in the world to discover that coal could be burnt, and today it is the main fuel source. Among other valuable mineral deposits, the north-west and north-east of China have rich oil reserves which are important for fuel and the chemical industry. Despite these resources there is still a problem supplying enough power to new industries and so China is trying alternative sources of energy such as **hydroelectric power**.

Engineers test-drilling in the deserts of north-west China. This area has rich mineral reserves.

Textiles are important, supplying both the Chinese and the export market. Apart from man-made fabrics, cotton and silk are two natural fibres processed in China. Silk cloth, which uses the thread of the silk worm cocoon, has been woven in China for hundreds of years.

Main exports:	Minerals, fuels, petroleum products, clothing and fabrics, food, animals
Main imports:	Machinery (especially for industry and transport) rolled steel, light industrial products, chemical fertilizers, plastics, rubber, timber

The manufacturing industry is the most important sector of China's industrial economy. Agricultural and industrial machinery are major products. Consumer goods, such as bicycles, televisions, household items and textiles, are in increasing demand as people's standard of living rises.

Recently China has opened its doors to foreign tourists. Tourism is a major growth industry and an important source of foreign currency.

A boy hand-painting a vase in a porcelain and china factory.

18 Transport

Whereas most families in the West have a car, the most popular form of private transport in China is the bicycle. There are millions of bicycles. To avoid accidents each side of the road in towns is divided into two, half for bicycles and half for lorries and buses. There are very few cars in China; they are either taxis or for the use of important officials.

Public transport is cheap and frequent, but trains, buses and boats are always crowded. For shorter distances in and between towns most people use buses. Because the road system is not very good and the distances between cities are so large, trains are used for longer journeys. Steam trains are still used in many parts of the country although they are gradually being replaced by diesel and electric trains.

The rivers of China have always been used to transport people and goods. In the thirteenth century the 1800-km Grand Canal was completed. It was the longest man-made waterway in the world, and linked Beijing to the two big rivers, the Huang He and the Chang Jiang. Parts of the canal are still **navigable** today.

Above Steam trains are still used in most parts of China, particularly for transporting goods.

Right Lorries carry goods to the remote parts of the country not served by railways.

Although bicycles are used in rural areas, most people walk to school or work. In Tibet people sometimes travel by yak, in Xinjiang camels are used, and in many parts of northern China people travel by horse-drawn carts or on horseback. Sometimes there is no bus service and so people travel in trucks or on a trailer behind a tractor.

There are over one hundred airports in China but flying is expensive, so the aeroplanes are mainly used by officials or foreigners.

Above *In north-west China carts are sometimes pulled by camels and donkeys.*

Below *This man is taking his vegetables to market on the back of his tricycle.*

19 Government

China is controlled by the Communist Party who make all policy decisions about how the country is run. The head of the Communist Party is called the General Secretary. Only about 1 in 20 of the total population are members of the Communist Party, although many other people support it as any different view on politics is not encouraged.

The **administration** of the country lies with the State Council, headed by the Premier. The heads of all the various government departments, such as education or defence, are all members of the State Council. Many of these officials are also members of the Communist Party.

Above As part of the drive against crime, pictures of criminals and descriptions of their crimes are often put up in public places.

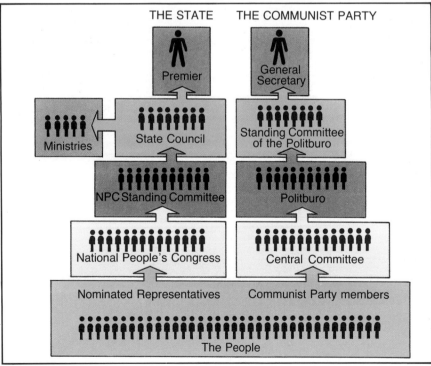

Left The structure of the Chinese Government. The Communist Party has the power and makes the decisions. The State runs the country based on the Communist Party's decisions.

Left A local policeman takes his daughter for a ride on his motorbike.

Below The Great Hall of the People, in Beijing, where the National People's Congress meets.

China is split into twenty-two provinces (including **Taiwan**), five **autonomous regions** and three **municipalities**. From the top level of government down to the work unit there are twenty-four levels of administration. The work units at the lowest level have considerable control over local matters, although Communist Party representatives make sure official policies are followed. Any official person with responsibility is called a *cadre*.

The People's Liberation Army, which was so important in helping to create the People's Republic of China, is still used by the Communist Party to maintain order, although the number of soldiers has been reduced in recent years.

China's written law is much less complicated than that of most countries. The police and **magistrates** enforce laws, but there is no jury. The death penalty still exists for major crimes. Small disputes over property or family matters are usually settled by local *cadres*.

20 Facing the future

Without a doubt, China's main concern for the future is the population explosion. If the size of the population is not controlled there will be food, housing and other shortages. The Government's aim is to limit the population to 1.2 billion by the year 2000, but it all depends on the success of the birth control policies.

Above Large posters on the street encourage families to have only one child.

Above Many young people are now learning practical skills. Chinese industry needs well-trained workers.

The Government also sees the modernization of industry as an important priority. Technology is slowly being improved with the help of equipment and expertise from foreign countries, such as Australia and Canada, but there are still not enough well-trained people in China who can use the new machines. So education, particularly technical and **vocational**, will also have to be improved.

The policy in China has been to give everyone a job. This now means that many industries are overmanned and that some people have little to do at work. Added to this some cities have an unemployment problem with a shortage of jobs for young people.

Now that Chinese people have more money they like to buy Western-style goods when they can, demanding a wider and wider choice of products.

How large this choice may become depends on the Communist leadership of the country.

In 1997, the British-controlled island of Hong Kong is due to be returned to China. It is a major world financial centre with a very different way of life from mainland China. Chinese people there are worried about their future under a Communist government, particularly in the light of recent unrest.

China has seen great progress over the last forty years and has the potential to become a leading developed nation in the future.

Right Young Chinese like to wear Western clothes and listen to pop music.

Below Hong Kong, an island which lies off the south coast of China, will return to Chinese control in 1997.

Glossary

Administration The people who carry out policies.

Ancestors The people from whom we are all descended such as grandparents and great-grandparents. The Chinese have always had great respect for their ancestors.

Autonomous regions These areas are partly self-governing; in China they are the areas in which many of the minority peoples live.

Barren Unable to grow crops.

Buddhists Followers of the Buddhist religion.

Ceramics The art and techniques of producing articles of clay and porcelain.

Domesticated Used to describe a wild animal that has been brought under human control.

Droughts Long periods with no rain.

Dynasties A series of rulers who come from the same family.

Endangered species Types of animals or birds of which there are very few left.

Expertise Special skill or knowledge.

Exploited To be taken advantage of by someone more powerful.

Famines Desperate shortages of food causing hunger and starvation.

Fertile (of soil) Very rich and nourishing, encouraging the growth of plants.

Forage To search for food.

Genghis Khan (1162-1227) A warrior from Mongolia whose armies conquered lands from China to Europe.

Hong Kong An island south of China controlled by the British since 1842 but to be returned to China in 1997. It is a modern financial and trading centre.

Hydroelectric power (HEP) Using water power to make electricity.

Isolated Set apart; separate from others.

Life expectancy The length of time people are expected to live.

Lunar months A period of time from one new moon to the next (approx. 28 days).

Magistrates People who have the power to enforce laws.

Marco Polo (c1254–c1324) An Italian merchant who travelled in China and later wrote about his travels.

Minority A group of people that is different in some way (for example, race, religion or politics) from a larger group of which it is a part.

Monsoon A strong wind which blows in from the sea in summer bringing heavy rains.

Municipalities Towns or cities; here it includes Beijing, Shanghai and Tianjin.

Muslims Followers of the Islamic religion.

Navigable Wide, deep or safe enough to be sailed on or through.

Nomadic Used to describe people who move from place to place to find grazing for their animals.

Noodles A food made of plain cooked wheat flour, rather like spaghetti.

Oases Areas in the middle of a desert where there is water and vegetation.

Pavilions Ornamental buildings.

Peasants People who work on the land; usually quite poor.

Philosopher Someone who searches for truth and wisdom; a deep thinker.

Pilgrimages Journeys to sacred or religious places.

Polluted Containing dangerously high levels of dirt and poisonous substances in the air or in water; usually produced by factories.

Porcelain White glazed china of especially fine quality.

Private enterprise A business run by an individual. Until recently the Chinese government did not allow this and everyone worked for government-run organizations.

Republic A country that has an elected leader instead of being ruled by a king, queen or emperor.
Revolutionary Taking part in bringing about a complete change in methods or outlook.
Salamander A newt-like animal that likes water.
Seismograph An instrument for measuring earth tremors caused by earthquakes.
Self-sufficient To be able to provide food and other needs without the help of others.
State farms Farms owned and run by the government.
Surplus More than is needed.
Syllable A sound that makes a word or part of a word (for example, the words *boy* and *girl* both have one syllable, but the words *women* and *children* each have two).

Taiwan This island off the coast of China was where Chiang Kai Shek fled from the Communists and set up another government. Even though it is not under the control of the Communist Government, it is considered a part of China.
Tomb A place where dead people are buried; usually a room underground.
Vocational Used to describe education or training which leads to a particular job or profession.
Warlords Strong military leaders.
Yak An ox with a thick, shaggy coat which keeps it warm in freezing weather; it only survives at high altitudes.

Books to read

Blackwood, Alan *Spotlight on the Rise of Modern China* (Wayland,1986)
China Features *We Live in China* (Wayland,1981).
Han, Suyin *Han Suyin's China* (Phaidon, 1987)
Jacobsen, Peter and Kristensen, Preben *A Family in China* (Wayland,1985).
Keeler, Stephen *Passport to China* (Franklin Watts,1987)
Merton, A. and Kan, Shio Yun *China: The Land and its People* (Macdonald,1986)

Money, D.C. *China: The Land and the People* (Evans Bros.,1984)
Moon, Bernice and Cliff *China is my Country* (Wayland,1983)
Shui, Yan Ming and Thompson, S. *Chinese Stories* (Wayland,1986)
Thompson S. and Shui, Amy *Chinese Food and Drink* (Wayland,1987)
Wood, Frances *People at Work in China* (Batsford,1987)
Wood Frances *Through the Year in China* (Batsford,1981)

Picture acknowledgements

All the photographs in this book were taken by Richard Sharpley with the exception of the following: Bruce Coleman Ltd 8 (top/Rod Williams), 8 (bottom/C.B. Frith), 9 (Gordon Langsbury); Peter Newark's Military Pictures 11, 12; Ronald Sheridan's Photo Library 10 (top/J.P. Stevens); Julia Waterlow 44.

Index